GREED

WHAT SOME PEOPLE ARE ABLE TO DO FOR MONEY.

VOLUME I.

Francesca & Flavio Fonti

FOR LAZY READERS

CRIME EDITION

GREED

WHAT SOME PEOPLE ARE ABLE TO DO FOR MONEY

VOLUME I.

FOR LAZY READERS PUBLISHING

This book was written, printed and bound
in the United States of America.

ISBN-13: 978-0984007004

ISBN-10: 0984007008

CONTACT

E mail: **info@forlazyreaders.com**

Website: **www.forlazyreaders.com**

TABLE OF CONTENTS:

STORIES

Some of the For Lazy Readers Series:

Business and Investing
Health, Mind and Body
Nonfiction
Millionaires
American Business
Biographies and Memoirs
Cooking, Food and Wine
Self-Help
Travel
Entertainment
Politics
Crime

Write For Lazy Readers Publishing

Our readers are looking for answers on nearly every part of their life.

For this reason we are looking for expert authors on all kinds of topics (see our series). If you are a topic expert with excellent writing skills and would like to contribute with some articles to FOR LAZY READERS, please go to **www.forlazyreaders.com** and complete the form.

We will review your credentials and writing sample and we will contact you.

Your writing sample submission is subject to the terms of conditions of use of the site. **Click here to review our terms and conditions.**

Thanks for your interest in working with For Lazy Readers Publishing

About For Lazy Readers Publishing

FOR LAZY READERS BOOK SERIES

have been started to help readers to inform about everyday topics, presenting even the most professional information difficult to understand about everything in plain English.

FOR LAZY READERS BOOK SERIES

are trying to present to the reader educational reference books and make difficult material interesting and easy. FLR are trying to explain any topic that's complex, often confusing and intimidating, or conjures up any feelings of anxiety.

What's more?

After positive feedback from our readers

FOR LAZY READERS BOOK SERIES

are available now in 2 languages, English and Spanish. We are preparing German and Italian editions.

FOR LAZY READERS BOOK SERIES

inform the reader about everything, for example: health, cooking, greed, scam, finances, corrupt politicians, taxes, travel destinations, different topics of business, celebrity businesses, exercise, weight loss, and more.

Gaining notice and garnering popularity quickly after the series introduction, we are just keeping expanding the selection.

We are working now in more topics.

Our books are great for individuals that just want to know the most important topics about everything in short format.

The diversity of this collection is held together by a common idea – the haunted life.

It's a funny and thoughtful collection of stories and it has a bit of everything.

This is a short story collection not short on ideas. It's one huge book of great, exciting stories, which will become a uniting force for readers of all forms of imaginative fiction.

This is a powerful, life affirming and boldly funny collection that everyone should experience.

About this book

GREED

WHAT SOME PEOPLE ARE ABLE TO DO FOR MONEY

VOLUME I.

Hysterical collection about actual stories and true crimes committed by "normal"people.

A short story collection.

Real criminal (court) stories of corruption and greed Volume I. - Crime Serie.

A collection of true crime stories from USA.

Greed is not limited to America.

Crime and punishment.

Follow with us the most recent criminal cases from the commission of the crime, thc arrest, the trial and the final judgment.

The book is focused on stories of greed about crimes such as insurance fraud, Ponzi schemes, credit card fraud, money laundering, identity theft, medical fraud, and more.

DEFINITION OF GREED

excessive or rapacious desire, especially for wealth or possessions.

Origin:
1600–10; back formation from greedy
Related forms
greed·less, *adjective*
greed·some, *adjective*

Some of the synonyms:
avarice, avidity, cupidity, covetousness; voracity, ravenousness, rapacity.

Greed, greediness denote an excessive, extreme desire for something, often more than one's proper share.
acquisitiveness, avarice, avidity, covetousness, craving, cupidity, eagerness, edacity, excess, gluttony, gormandizing, graspingness, hunger, indulgence, insatiableness, intemperance, longing, piggishness, rapacity, ravenousness, selfishness, swinishness, voracity.

By itself, this definition has no negative meaning; it's just as possible to be rationally greedy for something as irrationally greedy for it. However, it's become common to attach a negative connotation to it, just as is common with "selfish".

In Greek, the word was *philargyros*, lit. "money-loving."

A German word for it is *habsüchtig*, from *haben* "to have" + *sucht* "sickness, disease," with sense tending toward "passion for."

SOURCE: www.dictionary.com

GREED

SOME OF THE EFFECTS AND CAUSES OF THE GREED IN USA

GREED

-is the most serious problem today.
-drives U.S. into the ground.
-caused the disgraceful corporate scandals.
-is responsible for corrupted cops and politicians.
-causes worldwide sex slavery of women and children.
-drives the murders of the narcotics world.
-drives up food prices, causes starvation.
-is responsible for the exploitations of teen sports stars by colleges and for the mess in the pro sports world.
-is also the cause of the use of performance drugs by young athletes.
-is behind the scam artists who steal from the elderly.
-may have been a more serious problem for Americans, say, in the era of the robber barons.
-causes the constant efforts to destroy work unions that protect basic worker rights.
-has led to the incorrect immigration policy.
-has produced a lot of tax cuts that have provided more money to the rich and in effect taken it away from the poor.
-accounts for the efforts to take profitability out of the pensions and health insurance of working men and women.
-is responsible that so many Americans have no health insurance and is responsible of the fact that the recent reform of Medicare was a fraud.
-causes newspapers to overestimate their circulation.
-is responsible for the obscene salaries of CEOs of the biggest American corporations.
-is the cause of the high wages paid to the CEOs even if the company is going to bankrupt or failing.
-is responsible for the endless stress and ruthless competition of the workplace and the strains and tensions of professional class marriages.
-is responsible for outsourcing, which is incapable of comprehending that the employees who lose their jobs are also the consumers who sustain the

economy.
-generates the reckless ventures that in part caused not only the bubble of the late '90s.
-causes expensive wars that shatter our budget.
-is the reason that only the wealthy are benefiting so far.
-drives loan sharks that give away loans and credit cards with incredible high interest rate, that the people are not able to pay back.
-is responsible for the success of big box stores that tax the poor with low wages.
-is the reason poor white, Hispanics, African Americans or Native Americans must fight the wars that the wealthy start.

1.
Greedy Judge

"As time goes on we get closer to that American Dream of there being a pie cut up and shared. Usually greed and selfishness prevent that and there is always one bad apple in every barrel."

Rick Danko

2011, Scranton, PA

Mark A. Ciavarella, former president judge of the Court of Common Pleas and former judge of the Juvenile Court for Luzerne County, was sentenced in federal court in Scranton, Penn. by Senior U.S. District Court Judge Edwin M. Kosik II.

Senior Judge Kosik sentenced Ciavarella to 28 years in prison and ordered restitution be paid in the amount of $965,930 to the Commonwealth of Pennsylvania for his judicial salary and $207,861 in restitution related to the tax charges.

Ciavarella and his co-defendant, Michael Conahan, who also served as president judge of the Court of Common Pleas of Luzerne County, were initially charged in January 2009 with honest services mail and wire fraud and tax fraud in connection with the use of privately owned juvenile detention facilities. The charges were the result of a federal investigation of alleged corruption in the Luzerne County court system. The inquiry began in 2007 and over the next four years expanded to include county government offices, state legislators, school districts, and contractors in Northeastern Pennsylvania. Both defendants agreed to plead guilty. In July 2009, Judge Kosik rejected the proposed plea agreements because the defendants did not appear to accept responsibility for their conduct.

In September 2009 and September 2010, a grand jury in Harrisburg, Penn., returned superseding indictments charging both defendants with racketeering, honest services mail fraud, money laundering, extortion, bribery, tax violations, and conspiracy. The government also sought the forfeiture of approximately $2.8 million in assets allegedly acquired by the defendants through racketeering and money laundering. In response to the U.S. Supreme Court's 2010 decision in *United States v. Skilling*, the 2010 indictment specifically charged that bribes and kickbacks were paid to the defendants.

After an 11-day trial in Scranton in February 2011, a jury found Ciavarella guilty on 12 of 39 counts: racketeering, racketeering conspiracy, money laundering conspiracy, conspiracy to defraud the United States, four counts of honest services mail fraud, and four counts of filing false income tax returns. The jury also found that Ciavarella should forfeit $997,600, the sum he received from Robert Mericle, the developer who built the juvenile detention facilities.

Ciavarella testified at trial, claiming that the payments he received from

Mericle were "finders fees" or "honest money" with no connection to Ciavarella's actions as a judge, and denied that he received payment from Robert Powell, owner of the facilities.

The evidence established that Conahan closed the Luzerne County Juvenile Detention Facility when he was chief judge and helped arrange the financing for the private facilities; that Ciavarella, as juvenile court judge, sent juveniles to those facilities; that both men obstructed efforts to question the county's use of the facilities and their financial relationships with Mericle and Powell; and both judges used bank accounts, straw parties and real estate vacation property to hide and launder payments received from Mericle and Powell. The evidence also showed that Ciavarella failed to report receipt of the funds on annual financial interest statements he was required to file as a judge and failed to report the income on his federal income tax returns. Mericle and Powell have pleaded guilty pursuant to plea agreements and are awaiting sentencing.

Conahan pleaded guilty to racketeering conspiracy in April 2010. He did not testify at trial and has not been sentenced.

The judicial scandal, described as the worst in Pennsylvania's history, and the federal prosecutions have had major consequences: Ciavarella and Conahan resigned from the bench in 2009. Reform and housecleaning are underway in the Luzerne County court system. The Supreme Court of Pennsylvania was compelled to vacate thousands of juvenile convictions in Luzerne County as a result of Ciavarella's conduct as a juvenile court judge. A State Interbranch Commission on Juvenile Justice was established to study what happened and to recommend changes in the state's justice system aimed at safeguarding the constitutional rights of juveniles and improving the oversight and disciplinary process for judges in Pennsylvania.

In June 2011, a committee of the American Bar Association reviewed and made recommendations to improve procedures in the state's Judicial Conduct Board. A procedure was established in Luzerne County for compensation of victims of the activities of Ciavarella and Conahan.

Ciavarella voluntarily surrendered at the end of the sentencing hearing and was taken into custody by the U.S. Marshals.

In the U.S. Attorney's Office, the prosecution was conducted by a team consisting of Senor Litigation Counsel Gordon A.D. Zubrod, Assistant U.S. Attorneys William S. Houser, Michael A. Consiglio and Amy Phillips, and Criminal Division Chief Christian A. Fisanick.

Investigated by the agents of the Internal Revenue Service, Criminal Investigations and the FBI's Scranton office.

2.

Investigation of Political Corruption and International Money Laundering Rings Nets 44 Individuals

Anyway, no drug, not even alcohol, causes the fundamental ills of society. If we're looking for the source of our troubles, we shouldn't test people for drugs, we should test them for stupidity, ignorance, greed and love of power.

P. J. O'Rourke

2009, Newark, NJ

The mayors of Hoboken, Secaucus and Ridgefield, the Jersey City deputy mayor and council president, two state assemblymen, numerous other public officials and political figures and five rabbis from New York and New Jersey were among 44 individuals charged in a two-track federal investigation of public corruption and a high-volume, international money laundering conspiracy.

Among those charged in criminal Complaints are:

- Peter Cammarano III, the newly elected mayor of Hoboken and an attorney, charged with accepting $25,000 in cash bribes, including $10,000 from an undercover cooperating witness.

- L. Harvey Smith, a New Jersey Assemblyman and recent mayoral candidate in Jersey City, charged along with an aide of taking $15,000 in bribes to help get approvals from high-level state agency officials for building projects.

- Daniel Van Pelt, a New Jersey Assemblyman, charged with accepting a $10,000 bribe.

- Dennis Elwell, mayor of Secaucus, charged with taking a $10,000 cash bribe.

- Anthony Suarez, mayor of Ridgefield and an attorney, charged with agreeing to accept a $10,000 corrupt cash payment for his legal defense fund.

- Louis Manzo, the recent unsuccessful challenger in the Jersey City mayoral election and former state Assemblyman, and his brother and political advisor Robert Manzo, both with taking $27,500 in corrupt cash payments for use in Louis Manzo's campaign.

- Leona Beldini, the Jersey City deputy mayor and a campaign treasurer, charged with taking $20,000 in conduit campaign contributions and other self-dealing in her official capacity.

- Eliahu Ben Haim, of Long Branch, N.J., the principal rabbi of a synagogue in Deal, N.J., charged with money laundering of proceeds derived from criminal activity.

- Saul Kassin, of Brooklyn, N.Y., the chief rabbi of a synagogue in Brooklyn, New York, charged with money laundering of proceeds derived from criminal activity.

- Edmund Nahum, of Deal, N.J., the principal rabbi of a synagogue in

Deal, charged with money laundering of proceeds derived from criminal activity.

- Mordchai Fish, of Brooklyn, N.Y., a rabbi at a synagogue in Brooklyn, charged with money laundering of proceeds derived from criminal activity. His brother, also a rabbi, was charged as well.

Most of the defendants were arrested by a large contingent of federal agents, led by Special Agents of the FBI Newark Division and IRS Criminal Investigation Division. Court-authorized search warrants were also being executed approximately 20 locations in New Jersey and New York, to recover, among other things, large sums of cash and other evidence of criminal conduct. Additionally, 28 seizures warrants were being executed against bank accounts in the names of the money laundering defendants and entities they control.

One criminal Complaint charges a Brooklyn man, Levy Izhak Rosenbaum, with conspiring to broker the sale of a human kidney for a transplant, at a cost of $160,000 to the transplant recipient. According to the Complaint, Rosenbaum said he had been brokering the sale of kidneys for 10 years.

Those charged in the money laundering investigation, are scheduled to begin making initial appearances thereafter before U.S. Magistrate Judge Mark Falk.

Law enforcement personnel, with the assistance of a cooperating witness, first infiltrated a pre-existing money laundering network that operated internationally between Brooklyn, Deal, N.J. and Israel and laundered at least tens of millions of dollars through charitable, non-profit entities controlled by rabbis in New York and New Jersey.

The cooperating witness told targets of the money laundering investigation that he was involved in illegal businesses and bank frauds. He also openly discussed with targets that he was in bankruptcy and was attempting to conceal cash and assets, and told them he wanted to launder criminal proceeds in increments ranging from tens of thousands of dollars to $150,000 or more at a time, often at the rate of several transactions per week. According to the criminal Complaints, the money laundering operations run by the rabbis laundered a total of approximately $3 million for the cooperating witness alone between about June 2007 and July 2009.

The investigation veered onto its public corruption track in July 2007 in Hudson County, where the cooperating witness represented himself to be a developer and owner of a tile business who wanted to build high rises and other projects and get public contracts in Hudson County schools. Through an intermediary, the cooperating witness was introduced to a Jersey City building inspector who, in return for $40,000 in bribes, promised to smooth the way for approvals of the cooperating witness's building projects, according to the criminal Complaints.

From there, introductions and referrals spread amongst a web of public officials, council and mayoral candidates, their operatives and associates - mostly in Hudson County, and primarily in Jersey City - who took bribes. In return, they pledged their official assistance in getting the cooperating witness's projects prioritized and approved or to steer contracts to him.

In part, the bribe-taking was connected to fund raising efforts in heavily contested mayoral and city council campaigns in Jersey City and Hoboken, and the bribes were often parceled out to straw donors, who then wrote checks in their names or businesses to the campaigns in amounts that complied with legal limits on individual donations – so-called conduit or conversion donations. Other bribe recipients took cash for direct personal use and benefit; others kept some of the cash and used the rest for political campaigns, according to the criminal Complaints.

The investigation produced hundreds of hours of video and audio recordings documenting much of the money laundering and bribe-taking.

"This investigation has once again identified a corrupt network of public officials who were all too willing to take cash in exchange for promised official action," said Marra. "It seemed that everyone wanted a piece of the action. The corruption was widespread and pervasive."

"In both parts of this investigation," Marra said, "respected figures in positions of public and private trust engaged in conduct behind closed doors that belied the faces of honesty, integrity and rectitude they displayed daily to their respective constituencies."

"The list of names and titles of those arrested sounds like a roster for a community leaders meeting," said Weysan Dun, Special Agent In Charge of the FBI in Newark. "Sadly, these prominent individuals were not in a meeting room but were in the FBI booking room. We hope that our actions will be the clarion call that prompts significant change in the way business and politics are conducted in the State of New Jersey. Those who engage in this culture of corruption should know the cross hairs of justice will continue to be focused on them."

"Traditional money laundering used to be confined to narcotics traffickers and organized crime," said Julio La Rosa, Acting Special Agent in Charge of the IRS Criminal Investigation Division (CID). "Based on the allegations contained in today's complaints, money laundering has no boundaries and impacts every segment of our society."

The investigation is the third phase of the FBI, IRS-CID and U.S. Attorney's Office "Bid Rig" investigations that began first in Monmouth and Ocean counties in New Jersey.

The initial investigation became public in 2002 with the guilty plea of Ocean Township mayor Terrence Weldon, who admitted extorting cash from developers to influence approval of projects. The second Bid Rig phase resulted in the arrests in February 2005 of 11 sitting and former mayors and other elected officials in Monmouth County.

Those public officials took bribes from someone they believed was a contractor and money launderer seeking municipal work but who was, in fact, an undercover cooperating witness.

The Money Laundering Investigation

The money laundering conspiracy involved high-ranking religious figures and their associates in Brooklyn, N.Y. and Deal, N.J. Among them was Eliahu Ben Haim, of Long Branch, N.J., the principal rabbi of Congregation Ohel Yaacob in Deal, N.J. Typically, according to the criminal Complaints, Haim received bank checks in amounts ranging from tens of thousands of dollars up to $160,000 at a time made payable to a charitable, tax-exempt organization associated with Haim and his synagogue. To complete the money laundering cycle, Haim would return the amount of the check in cash to the cooperating witness, less a cut for Haim, typically 10 percent.

Haim's source of cash for funding the money laundering was, according to the Complaints, an Israeli in Israel who, Haim said, he had worked with for years. For a fee, that source would make cash available through other individuals who ran cash houses in Brooklyn. Hundreds of thousands of dollars were regularly available from the cash houses for Haim to return to his money-laundering clients, including the government's cooperating witness.

Similar circles of money launderers in Brooklyn and Deal, N.J. operated separately but occasionally co-mingled activities and participants. In most cases, the rings were led by rabbis who used charitable, non-profit entities connected to their synagogues to "wash" money that they understood came from criminal activity like bank fraud, counterfeit goods and other illegal sources, according to the criminal Complaints. Since such large amounts of cash were being transacted—tens to hundreds of thousands of dollars per transaction, often multiple times in a week—the rabbis made significant sums in fees, which typically ran between five and ten percent per transaction.

One of the other money laundering operations was allegedly led by Saul Kassin, a leading Brooklyn rabbi, and another by Edmund Nahum, the leader of a synagogue in Deal. In one secretly recorded conversation, Nahum tells the cooperating witness that he should launder his money through a number of rabbis. "The more it's spread the better," Nahum said, according to his criminal Complaint.

In another conversation, Kassin allegedly asked the cooperating witness—who at the moment was conducting a $25,000 transaction with Kassin—why he didn't do all his business with Haim. The cooperating witness replied that he had by that time already conducted between $600,000 and $700,000 in money laundering transactions with Haim.

Another group of alleged money launderers was led by Mordchai Fish, a rabbi at a Brooklyn synagogue. Fish's brother, Lavel Schwartz, a rabbi, was also charged with money laundering.

Levi Deutsch was also arrested, an Israeli living in Israel who, according to the Complaints, was a high-level source of cash from overseas for funding the bank checks that passed through charitable entities. Deutsch, who traveled frequently between Israel and New York, explained to the cooperating witness that the source of his cash was the "diamond business (and) other, other things," according to the Complaints.

He further explained that he was associated with a Swiss banker who charged "two, three points" per $1 million laundered through him. (Deutsch is a different person than the Israeli working with Haim.)

Finally, another alleged money launderer was Moshe "Michael" Altman, a Hudson County real estate developer who, according to the criminal Complaints, "washed" more than $600,000 in dirty checks to cash for the cooperating witness through charitable, non-profit entities. Altman is also the intermediary who introduced the cooperating witness to Jersey City building inspector John Guarini, who allegedly took $20,000 from the cooperating witness in July 2007, and $40,000 in total over time. That initial bribe is what gave rise to the public corruption portion of the investigation.

The Public Corruption Investigation

Guarini introduced the cooperating witness to Maher A. Khalil, deputy director of the Jersey City Department of Health and Human Services and a former member of the Jersey City Zoning Board of Adjustment. Khalil - who accepted $30,000 in cash payments from the cooperating witness - made key referrals that set in motion a kind of "corruption networking" amongst the defendants as well as others, Marra said.

Introductions usually took place at diners and restaurants in Jersey City, Bayonne, Weehawken, Hoboken, Staten Island, Toms River, Atlantic City and elsewhere. Envelopes stuffed with cash were often passed from the cooperating witness to recipients or their intermediaries in parking lots after such meetings, according to the criminal Complaints.

Khalil pledged to the cooperating witness to make introductions only to "players" who would "do the right thing" by approving the cooperating witness's development plans in exchange for payments, according to his criminal Complaint. All along the way, each of the individuals charged allegedly took cash bribes up to $20,000 at a time - often numerous times - either taking the money outright or scheming to direct conduit payments through others to political campaigns in Jersey City or Hoboken. In each instance, the defendants acknowledged that, in exchange for the cash or cash campaign contributions, they would vote for and/or use their official influence to expedite and get approvals for the cooperating witness's projects.

Following are the individuals charged in the public corruption investigation, with the exception of Khalil and Guarini above, and summaries of their alleged conduct from the criminal Complaints:

- Leona Beldini, deputy mayor of Jersey City and a realtor. Beldini planned to become broker for his purported 750-unit condominium project on Garfield Avenue, where units would sell for $500,000 each. Beldini, who was treasurer of a Jersey City official's re-election campaign (that official is identified only as Jersey City Official 4 in the Complaints), also accepted $20,000 in campaign donations, which she said would be divided between "donors" who would return the money to the campaign in increments of $2,600, the maximum individual donation allowed under law.

- Jack M. Shaw, a Hudson County political consultant. As described in the Complaint, he took $10,000 from the cooperating witness for himself and proposed that the cooperating witness pay $10,000 in campaign contributions for the re-election campaign of Jersey City Official 4.

- Edward Cheatam, the affirmative action officer for Hudson County, a commissioner with the Jersey City Housing Authority and, until May, vice president of the Jersey City Board of Education. Cheatam took $15,000 in cash bribes. (Khalil had introduced Cheatam to the cooperating witness; Cheatam then introduced Beldini and Shaw to the cooperating witness, all of whom then went on to extend introductions of the cooperating witness to many others.)

- Mariano Vega, Jr., the Jersey City council president. He met several times with the cooperating witness and ultimately accepted three $10,000 payments, two of which Vega instructed an intermediary to have broken down and converted into individual contributions for his re-election campaign and the third which he received after his election victory.

- Louis Manzo, a defeated candidate for Jersey City mayor, and his brother and political advisor, Ronald. Together, they accepted $27,500 in three cash payments intended for Louis Manzo's campaign. The cooperating witness was told that giving money to Louis Manzo was "insurance" to secure his influence for the cooperating witness in the event the incumbent for mayor lost.

- Lavern Webb-Washington, an unsuccessful candidate for the Jersey City council and a self-described housing activist. She accepted $15,000 in three cash installments of $5,000 for her political campaign.

- Lori Serrano, an unsuccessful candidate for the Jersey City council and former chair of the Jersey City Housing Authority. Serrano accepted $10,000 in two cash payments of $5,000 for her political campaign.

- James P. King, an unsuccessful candidate for Jersey City Council, former head of the Jersey City Parking Authority, former chairman of the Jersey City Incinerator Authority and a former Hudson County undersheriff. He accepted two payments of $5,000 each for his political campaign.

- Michael J. Manzo (no relation to the other Manzos), an unsuccessful candidate for Jersey City Council, and a Jersey City arson investigator. He agreed to accept a $5,000 cash payment from the cooperating witness for his campaign.

- Joseph Castagna, a health officer with the Jersey City Department of

Health and Human Services, and a close associate of Michael Manzo. Castagna took the $5,000 payment from the cooperating witness to pass to Michael Manzo.

- Dennis Jaslow, an investigator for the Hudson County Board of Elections and formerly a state corrections officer. Jaslow accepted $2,500, but complained that he wanted $5,000.

- Joseph Cardwell, a political consultant and a commissioner of the Jersey City Municipal Utilities Authority. He accepted two payments of $10,000 in cash to assist the cooperating witness with local government officials in Jersey City and other municipalities, and another $10,000, most of which was used for the purchase of fundraising event tickets.

- Guy Catrillo, a Jersey City planning aide and member of the mayor's "Action Bureau," and an unsuccessful candidate for the city council. Catrillo took $10,000 in campaign cash and another $5,000.

- L. Harvey Smith, state Assemblyman, a Jersey City mayoral candidate and former three-term councilman in Jersey City and a Hudson County undersheriff. Smith took two cash payments, one for $5,000, the other for $10,000, in exchange for approaching high-level contacts with the state Department of Transportation and Department of Environmental Protection to clear the way for approvals of the cooperating witness's project on Garfield Avenue in Jersey City and another project off Route 440 in Bayonne. Smith's aide, Richard Greene, is charged in the same criminal Complaint, and is accused of taking the $5,000 payment from the cooperating witness and passing it to Smith.

- Peter Cammarano III, previously a Hoboken councilman and now mayor, and a lawyer specializing in election law. While a candidate for mayor, then-councilman Cammarano and his close associate, Michael Schaffer, a commissioner on the North Hudson Utilities Authority, took three payments of $5,000 each with the promise that, in return, Cammarano would sponsor zoning changes and push through building plans for high-rise development in Hoboken by the cooperating witness. After the conclusion of their first meeting at a Hoboken diner, the cooperating witness stated, "Make sure you get my stuff expedited." To which Cammarano replied: "I promise you ... you're gonna be treated like a friend." Moments later, in the parking lot, Schaffer took the first $5,000 in cash. On July 16, Cammarano and Schaffer met the cooperating witness again at a Hoboken diner and accepted another $10,000, which Cammarano said was needed to pay campaign debts, bringing the total in bribes accepted by Cammarano and Schaffer to $25,000.

- Dennis Elwell, mayor of Secaucus, and Ronald Manzo (Manzo is charged in this Complaint in addition to the one with his brother Louis). Elwell received a $10,000 cash bribe—through Manzo as the middleman—to assist the cooperating witness with plans to build a hotel in Secaucus. Manzo took $5,000 from the cooperating witness as a reward for bringing Elwell to him.

- Anthony Suarez, mayor of Ridgefield Borough and an attorney, and co-defendant Vincent Tabbachino, owner of a tax preparation business in Guttenberg. Suarez accepted $10,000 from the cooperating witness through Tabbachino as a middleman, for Suarez's promised assistance in getting approvals to develop properties in Ridgefield. Tabbachino said he kept the cash and, in turn, would write checks totaling $10,000 (one check for $2,500 was cashed) to a legal defense fund for Suarez related to an allegation made by a political opponent of Suarez. Tabbachino also laundered $100,000 in cash from the cooperating witness's purported knock-off handbag business.

- Daniel M. Van Pelt, state Assemblyman and administrator for Lumberton Township. Van Pelt accepted $10,000 from the cooperating witness for his influence as a state Assemblyman to help in getting the necessary permits for a purported project the cooperating witness was planning in Waretown, Ocean Township. Van Pelt particularly offered his influence in obtaining the necessary permits from the state Department of Environmental Protection.

- Jeffrey Williamson, a Lakewood housing inspector, who was also a state Assembly candidate in 2007. He accepted a total of more than $16,000 in bribes in regular payments of $1,000 between about May 2007 and July 2011, to provide lenient inspections on rental and other properties owned by the cooperating witness in Lakewood. Williamson also allowed the cooperating witness to illegally use a residence in Lakewood as a commercial office. Charles "Shaul" Amon aided in the Lakewood payoff scheme by introducing Williamson to the cooperating witness. Charles "Shaul" Amon, previously worked for the cooperating witness managing properties in Lakewood. Amon aided in the Lakewood payoff scheme by introducing Williamson to the cooperating witness. Amon described how he had previously made payoffs to Williamson to go light on housing inspections.

The Money Laundering Defendants

Following are the individuals charged in the money laundering investigation and summaries of their alleged conduct as described in the criminal Complaints (All defendants are presumed innocent unless proven guilty beyond a reasonable doubt):

- Saul Kassin, the chief rabbi of Sharee Zion in Brooklyn, who laundered more than $200,000 with the cooperating witness between June 2007 and December 2008 by accepting "dirty" bank checks from the cooperating witness and exchanging them for clean checks from Kassin's charitable organization, after taking a fee of 10 percent for each transaction.

- Edmund Nahum, principal rabbi at Deal Synagogue in Deal, N.J., who laundered money both acting alone and with Kassin. Nahum laundered $185,000 between June 2007 and December 2008 by accepting dirty checks from the cooperating witness and exchanging them for clean checks from his own and Kassin's charitable organizations, after taking a fee of 10 percent for each transaction. Both Kassin and Nahum also laundered money to create fictitious tax deductions by accepting checks made payable to their charitable organizations, which created the appearance of charitable donations. They then deducted their 10 percent fee for laundering the checks through their charitable organization accounts and returned to the originators checks drawn on one of their accounts for 90 percent of the value of the original checks. These return checks would be payable to a name designated by the originators.

- Eli Ben Haim, principal rabbi of Congregation Ohel Yaacob in Deal, N.J., laundered $1.5 million with the cooperating witness between June 2007 and February 2009 by accepting dirty checks from the cooperating witness and exchanging them for cash, after taking a fee of approximately 10 percent for each transaction. His source for the cash was an Israeli who, for a fee of 1.5 percent, supplied the cash through intermediary cash houses run by defendants Weiss, Ehrental, and Cohen, who are described below. Ben Haim remarked that at one time he had laundered between $7 million and $8 million in one year, and earned $1 million laundering money in that year.

Cash House Operators for Haim Transactions:

- Arye Weiss—operated cash house from his residence in Brooklyn for Haim money laundering transactions; charged with supplying $300,000 in cash.

- Yeshayahu Ehrental—operated cash house from his office in Brooklyn for Haim money laundering transactions; charged with supplying $300,000 in cash.

- Schmulik Cohen—operated cash house from his residence in Brooklyn for Haim money laundering transactions; charged with supplying $850,000 in cash.

- Mordchai Fish—Rabbi of Congregation Sheves Achim in Brooklyn. Working with his brother Lavel Schwartz, also a rabbi in Brooklyn, Fish laundered approximately $585,000 with the cooperating witness by accepting dirty checks and exchanging them for cash, after taking a fee of 15 percent for each transaction. His source for the cash for some of the transactions was Levi Deutsch, who supplied the cash through an intermediary cash house run by Spira; for other transactions his source for the cash is unidentified but the cash was provided by cash couriers Gertner and Goldhirsh and cash houses run by Pollack and Weber. On two occasions over the course of his dealings with the Cooperating witness, Fish gave the Cooperating witness new chips for his cell phone to thwart any law enforcement attempt to wiretap their telephone calls.

- Levi Deutsch—Israeli source/supplier of cash for a number of Fish money laundering transactions. For a fee of two or three percent, he supplied cash for the transactions through intermediary Spira's cash house and is charged with supplying $200,000 in cash.

Cash House Operators and Cash Couriers for Fish Transactions:

- Binyomin Spira—operated a cash house from a bakery in Brooklyn in which he received cash from Levi Deutsch and supplied cash for Fish money laundering transactions, charged with supplying $200,000 in cash.

- Yolie Gertner—acted as a cash courier for Fish money laundering transactions, charged with moving $185,000 in cash.

- David Goldhirsh—acted as a cash courier for Fish money laundering transactions, charged with moving $100,000 in cash.

- Abe Pollack—operated cash house from his office in Brooklyn (which he shared with Naftoly Weber) for Fish money laundering transactions, charged with supplying $125,000 in cash.

- Naftoly Weber—operated cash house from his office in Brooklyn (which he shared with Abe Pollack) for Fish money laundering transactions, charged with supplying $125,000 in cash.

Additionally, money-laundering charges were filed against Shimon Haber and Itzak Friedlander, associates of Michael Altman.

Marra credited Special Agents of the FBI Red Bank Resident Agency, under the direction of Special Agent in Charge Weysan Dun, in Newark, and the IRS Criminal Investigation Division, under the direction of Acting Special Agent in Charge Julio La Rosa, for their commitment of resources and success in the Bid Rig cases to date. Marra also thanked the Monmouth County Prosecutor's Office under the direction of Prosecutor Luis Valentin for its assistance in the Bid Rig investigations.

Prosecuted by Brian Howe, Deputy Chief of the Special Prosecutions Unit, and Assistant U.S. Attorneys Mark McCarren, Sandra Moser and Maureen Nakly, all of the Special Prosecutions Division.

3.
Cheating Foster Parents

In our daily life, we encounter people who are angry, deceitful, intent only on satisfying their own needs. There is so much anger, distrust, greed, and pettiness that we are losing our capacity to work well together.

Margaret J. Wheatley

2011, Tampa, FL

It's almost unthinkable, parents stealing from their own foster child. But here's a story about a couple that did exactly that.

It's also a case that Tampa FBI Agent Dan Kelly, Florida Department of Law Enforcement Agent Terry Corn, and Acting U.S. Attorney Robert O'Neill won't soon forget. Said Kelly, "For financial crime investigations, we often don't get to know the victims, but in this instance, it was hard not to be absorbed into this boy's situation."

It started back in 2000, when 13-year-old Markus Kim suffered an unimaginable loss - his father murdered his mother. Markus was eventually placed with foster parents Radhames and Asia Oropeza in Flushing, New York.

About six months later, Markus learned he was entitled to a $500,000 life insurance policy that his mother had taken out. He couldn't access the money until he turned 18... in the interim it would be managed by the life insurance company. Not long after, Radhames and Asia Oropeza began suggesting that Markus consider real estate investing when he became of age.

Around the time Markus turned 18, his foster parents left New York without a word to him. Turns out they had moved to Florida, and about a year later, he was invited down to visit them. The Oropezas convinced their foster son to buy two $200,000 certificates of deposit (CDs) from a local bank... to better protect his money, they said. Because Markus trusted them, he followed their advice, and even allowed Asia Oropeza to co-sign bank documents.

The bank told Markus he'd receive monthly $1,000 checks—interest earned by the CDs. But after two checks, they stopped coming. He discovered that the CD accounts had been emptied and closed by Asia Oropeza.

So how did the FBI become involved? Markus, becoming exceedingly frustrated, contacted a legal aid attorney in New York, who in turn sought the help of an attorney in Florida. The attorney, who worked the case pro bono, contacted Acting U.S. Attorney O'Neill in Tampa. And O'Neill got in touch with the FBI and the Florida Department of Law Enforcement.

Our investigation revealed that the couple used the CDs - which were also in Asia Oropeza's name - as collateral when applying for two separate mortgage loans, and then once the CDs matured, they used the funds to pay off those loans.

Outcome. Asia Oropeza pled guilty to fraud, while her husband was later convicted at trial. They were ordered to pay Markus restitution, had their real estate holdings seized, and received prison terms.

During a press conference attended by investigators and prosecutors who worked the case, the 25-year-old Markus, who works as a concert stagehand in New York, received full restitution - a check for $409,662.07. He told the press that receiving the money gave him "a new lease on life."

Special Agent Kelly says that the investigation brought him and everyone else involved a great deal of satisfaction. "Cases like this," he explained, "show us what kind of impact our work actually has, and that's what keeps us out there doing it every day."

U.S. Attorney Robert E. O'Neill announced the major recovery of assets in a case involving a former foster child defrauded by his foster parents. According to court documents, Radhames Antonio Oropeza (54, Davenport, Polk County) and Asia Concepcion Oropeza (53, also of Davenport) acted as foster parents for Markus Min Ho Kim and then swindled more than $400,000 from him.

Kim came to the United States from Seoul, South Korea, with his natural parents at the age of 5. They lived in New York City. In 2000, Kim's natural father was charged and later convicted for the murder of Markus' mother and he was subsequently placed in the foster care system in New York.

Thereafter, Kim was placed in the foster care of Radhames Antonio Oropeza and Asia Oropeza. At the time of her death, Kim's mother had a life insurance policy for approximately $500,000. Kim was the beneficiary. Although he received the money upon her death, he could not access the funds until attaining the age of 18.

Upon turning 18 years of age, Kim received the proceeds from the policy. The Oropezas then conspired together to defraud Kim of the money and succeeded in depriving him of approximately $400,000. The Oropezas, who had moved to Polk County, Florida, used the proceeds to purchase real estate in Polk County. According to evidence presented at trial, the Oropezas funneled the money into certificates of deposits and later withdrew large amounts, then transferring them into alleged investment properties for Kim, to which he had no direct access.

Following a jury trial, on October 5, 2010 Radhames Oropeza was convicted of conspiracy to commit wire fraud. He was sentenced to 36 months in federal prison. Asia Oropeza pleaded guilty to the charges of conspiracy to commit wire fraud and wire fraud, prior to the start of the trial on October 4, 2010. She was sentenced to a term of 36 months in federal prison. Together Radhames and Asia Oropeza were ordered to pay restitution in the amount of $409,586.07 to Markus Min Ho Kim.

The Asset Recovery and Victim Rights Division of the United States Attorney's Office, Middle District of Florida was able to effectively recover $409,662.94 representing the total amount of restitution, plus interest, for the victim.

Investigated by the Federal Bureau of Investigation and the Florida Department of Law Enforcement. Prosecuted by United States Attorney Robert E. O'Neill.

4.
Investment Scam

I think one of the most pervasive evils in this world is greed and acquiring money for money's sake. Once you have six houses and a plane, it's just about a number. It's never been anything I understood.

Kevin Bacon

2011, Tampa, FL

United States Attorney Robert E. O'Neill announced that John S. Morgan (52, Sarasota) pleaded guilty to conspiracy to commit various crimes associated with a fraudulent investment scheme and money laundering. Morgan faces a maximum penalty of five years in federal prison on the conspiracy charge and 10 years on the money laundering charge.

According to the plea agreement, from about March 2005 through August 2009, John S. Morgan, his wife Marian I. Morgan and others perpetrated an investment fraud scheme through a Danish entity, which the Morgans had formed named Morgan European Holdings APS ("MEH"). MEH was purportedly in the business of investments commonly called "rime bank instrument trading programs." John Morgan knew that such programs did not exist; indeed, never engaged in such trading, and never met with a trader engaged in such trading. John Morgan and others nevertheless falsely represented to investors that MEH trading programs would yield returns of 30-70 percent per month or 200 percent per 90-120 day period, and that the investors' funds would never be put at risk.

He, along with others, explicitly promised investors that their funds would be held in escrow in a Danske Bank account for MEH and maintained by Danish attorney Eli Hecksher, who has been charged as a co-conspirator in the scheme. Instead of safeguarding the investor funds in escrow, John Morgan and others disposed of the funds by: 1) paying fees and expenses associated with the fraud; 2) providing refunds of principal to select investors; and 3) stealing and converting monies for their own personal benefit.

When investors did not receive the promised investment returns, and became concerned about the trading program, John Morgan and others provided a litany of excuses, assuring the investors that their funds were still on deposit and the delays were caused by circumstances beyond their control.

In all, John Morgan and others caused investors to transfer more than $27 million to MEH accounts. Approximately $10.7 million of this total was then used by John Morgan and others for their personal benefit.

Investigated by the Federal Bureau of Investigation and the Internal Revenue Service-Criminal Investigation. Prosecuted by Assistant United States Attorneys Cherie L. Krigsman and Robert T. Monk

5.
St. Petersburg Police Department Detective Indicted

There is something perverse about more than enough. When we have more, it is never enough. It is always somewhere out there, just out of reach. The more we acquire, the more elusive enough becomes.

Unknown

2011, Tampa, FL

United States Attorney Robert E. O'Neill announces the return of a seven-count indictment by a grand jury charging Anthony V. Foster (39, St. Petersburg) with public corruption charges. Counts one through six charges Foster with a wire fraud scheme to deprive the public of honest services. Count seven charges Foster with attempted extortion under color of official right. If convicted, Foster faces a maximum penalty of 20 years in federal prison, per count. The indictment also notifies Foster that the United States intends to forfeit $7,400 and a Samsung Television, which are alleged to be traceable to proceeds of the offense.

Foster was first arrested pursuant to a federal complaint on June 8, 2011. According to the charging documents, Foster, who worked as a detective for the St. Petersburg Police Department (SPPD), told one of his sources that he would contact state authorities involved in the source's state criminal cases to provide positive information about the source in exchange for Foster's personal receipt of cash and property payments. Sometime thereafter, Foster and the source met so that Foster could secure cash and property payments from the source. According to the indictment, Foster sent and received text messages to coordinate the meetings with the source.

The indictment also alleges that Foster contacted state authorities involved with the source's state criminal cases, identified himself as a detective with the SPPD, and provided positive information about the source's involvement in various SPPD investigations.

The indictment further alleges that Foster caused other SPPD officials to also contact state authorities on behalf of the source.

An indictment is merely a formal charge that a defendant has committed a violation of the federal criminal laws, and every defendant is presumed innocent unless, and until, proven guilty.

Investigated by the Federal Bureau of Investigation. Prosecuted by Assistant United States Attorney Jay G. Trezevant.

6.
$25 Million Medicare Fraud Scheme

There is enough in the world for everyone's need,
but not enough for everyone's greed.

Frank Buchman

2011, Miami, FL

A patient recruiter for a Miami health care agency pleaded guilty to his participation in a $25 million home health Medicare fraud scheme, announced the Department of Justice, the FBI and the Department of Health and Human Services (HHS).

Vicente Guerra-Nistal, 54, pleaded guilty before U.S. District Judge Joan A. Lenard in Miami to one count of conspiracy to commit health care fraud. Guerra was charged in a February 2011 indictment. According to plea documents, Guerra was a patient recruiter for ABC Home Health Care Inc. ABC was a Miami home health care agency that purported to provide home health and physical therapy services to Medicare beneficiaries.

According to court documents, ABC was operated for the purpose of billing the Medicare program for expensive physical therapy and home health care services that were medically unnecessary and/or were never provided. Court documents allege that the medically unnecessary services were prescribed by doctors, including Jose Nunez, M.D., and Francisco Gonzalez, M.D. Nunez and Gonzalez were also charged in the February 2011 indictment along with Guerra, and 18 other co-conspirators.

According to court documents, beginning in approximately January 2006, and continuing until approximately March 2009, Guerra offered and paid kickbacks and bribes to Medicare beneficiaries in return for those beneficiaries allowing ABC to bill Medicare for home health care and therapy services that were medically unnecessary and/or never provided. Guerra was paid kickbacks and bribes by the owners of ABC in return for recruiting the Medicare beneficiaries to ABC. Guerra admitted that he knew the patients he recruited for ABC did not qualify for the services that ABC billed to Medicare.

In addition, Guerra knew that the patient files for his recruited patients were falsified in order to make it appear that the patients qualified for home health care and therapy services so that Medicare could be billed for medically unnecessary services.

As a result of Guerra's participation in the illegal scheme, the Medicare program was billed approximately $194,000 for purported home health care services that were medically unnecessary and/or were never provided.

The charge of conspiracy to commit health care fraud carries a maximum prison sentence of 10 years. The defendant also face fines and terms of supervised release, as well as forfeiture of any property or proceeds derived from his criminal activities.

Co-defendants Lisandra Alonso and Luisa Morciego pleaded guilty for their roles in the fraud scheme on July 13, 2011. An indictment is merely a charge and defendants are presumed innocent until proven guilty.

Charges were announced by Assistant Attorney General Lanny A. Breuer of the Criminal Division; U.S. Attorney Wifredo A. Ferrer of the Southern District of Florida; John V. Gillies, Special Agent in Charge of the FBI's Miami Field Office; and Special Agent in Charge Christopher Dennis of the HHS Office of Inspector General (HHS-OIG), Office of Investigations Miami office.

Prosecuted by Trial Attorney Joseph S. Beemsterboer of the Criminal Division's Fraud Section. Investigated by the FBI and HHS-OIG, and was brought as part of the Medicare Fraud Strike Force, supervised by the Criminal Division's Fraud Section and the U.S. Attorney's Office for the Southern District of Miami.

Since their inception in March 2007, Medicare Fraud Strike Force operations in nine locations have charged more than 1,000 defendants who collectively have falsely billed the Medicare program for more than $2.3 billion. In addition, the HHS Centers for Medicare and Medicaid Services, working in conjunction with the HHS-OIG, are taking steps to increase accountability and decrease the presence of fraudulent providers.

FOR LAZY READERS

ABOUT AUTHORS

Flavio and Francesca Fonti

have been interested in writing short stories related with many different topics over many years. Both writers and businessmen are actively involved in publicizing new materials as a part of the FOR LAZY READERS SERIES. They are living in Florida.

FOR LAZY READERS

EDITIONS:

OUR SERIES

Business and Investing
Health, Mind and Body
Nonfiction
Millionaires
American Business
Biographies and Memoirs
Cooking, Food and Wine
Self-Help
Travel
Entertainment
Politics
Crime

For Lazy Readers Series in progress:

Crime Serie

GREED - What some people are able to do for money.

Volume II. and III.

SCAM - Be smart and protect yourself against scam.

Volume I., II., and III.

Health, Mind and Body Serie

HEALTH – How to live healthy and stop dieting.

Volume I. and II.

Millionaires Serie

TV REALITY SHOW – Reality that you don't know.

Volume I. and II.

American Business Serie

CELEBRITY ENTREPRENEURS - Facts you don't know about them. Volume I. and II.

More on **www.forlazyreaders.com**

Made in the USA
Monee, IL
04 November 2026

67384442R00036